The World's Deadliest

The Deadliest Weather

on Earth

by Connie Colwell Miller

www.raintreepublishers.co.uk
Visit our website to find out
more information about
Raintree books.

To order:
☎ Phone 0845 6044371
🖷 Fax +44 (0) 1865 312263
🖳 Email myorders@raintreepublishers.co.uk

Customers from outside the UK please telephone +44 1865 312262

Raintree is an imprint of Capstone Global
Library Limited, a company incorporated
in England and Wales having its registered
office at 7 Pilgrim Street, London,
EC4V 6LB – Registered company number:
6695582

Text © Capstone Press 2010
First published in hardback in the United
Kingdom by Capstone Global Library in 2011
The moral rights of the proprietor have
been asserted.

Edited by Abby Czeskleba
Designed by Matt Bruning
Media research by Svetlana Zhurkin
Production by Laura Manthe
Originated by Capstone Global Library Ltd
Printed and bound in China by South China
Printing Company Ltd

ISBN 978 1 406 21833 6
14 13 12 11 10
10 9 8 7 6 5 4 3 2 1

**British Library Cataloguing in Publication
Data**
Miller, Connie Colwell,
The deadliest weather on Earth. -- (The world's
deadliest)
551.6-dc22
A full catalogue record for this book is available
from the British Library.

Acknowledgements
We would like to thank the following for
permission to reproduce photographs:
Alamy pp. **7** (Royal Geographical Society),
11 (Mark Romesser), **13** (A. T. Willett), **17**
(Icelandic Photo Agency), **21** (Jon Arnold
Images), **29** (© Frantisek Staud); Getty
Images pp. **5** (Stone/Charles Doswell III), **15**
(Reportage/Mike Goldwater), **23** (Stone/Alan
R. Moller), **25** (Riser Angelo Cavalli); NASA
p. **27**; Shutterstock pp. **9** (Samuel Acosta), **19**
(Jhaz Photography).

Cover photograph of a tornado reproduced
with permission of Getty Images (Stone/Alan
R. Moller).

CONTENTS

Some words are printed in bold, **like this**. You can find out what they mean on page 30. You can also look in the box at the bottom of the page where they first appear.

DEADLY WEATHER

Every year, thousands of people around the world die in severe weather. Get ready to learn about some of the deadliest weather on the planet!

SLIGHTLY DANGEROUS

THAT BITES!

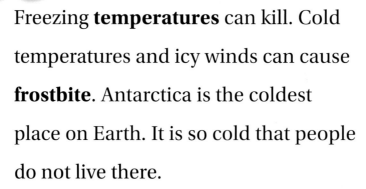

Freezing **temperatures** can kill. Cold temperatures and icy winds can cause **frostbite**. Antarctica is the coldest place on Earth. It is so cold that people do not live there.

frostbite when cold temperatures freeze the skin

temperature how hot or cold something is

DAMA

DEADLY FACT
People have lost fingers and toes with frostbite.

WILD WINDS

Strong winds knock down trees. Falling trees can hit cars, houses, and people. Powerful winds whip up dust and sand into wicked storms. Windblown dust and sand make it difficult to breathe and can even kill.

DEADLY FACT

Severe winds swept across Europe in 2007. People saw parked cars moving and lamp posts swaying in Swansea, Wales.

HAIL!

Chunks of ice called hail sometimes fall in thunderstorms. Small hailstones can damage cars, homes, and crops. Large hailstones can injure or even kill people and animals.

DEADLY FACT

Some hailstones are as large as cricket balls!

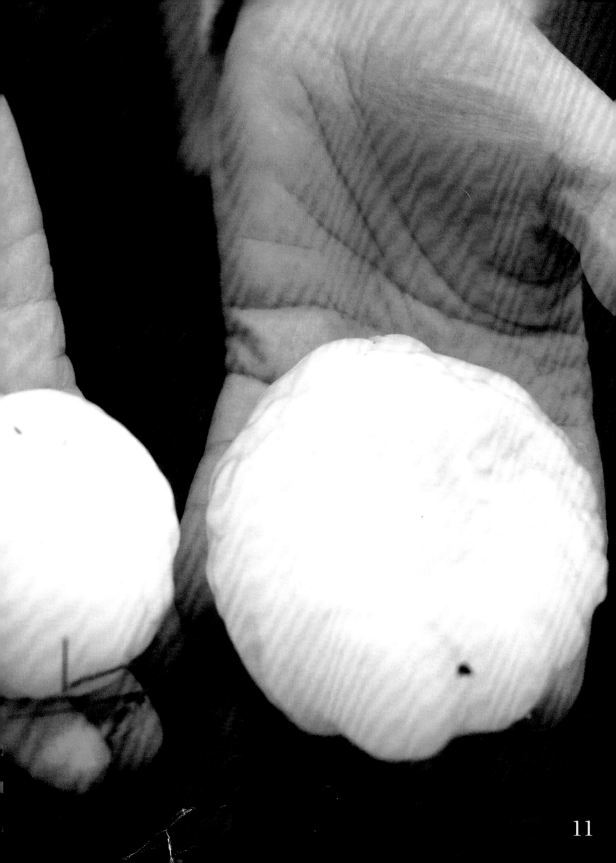

IN A FLASH

Heavy rains can cause **flash floods** in a short time. The rising water quickly sweeps cars off roads and covers homes. In the twentieth century, floods killed at least eight million people.

DEADLY *FACT*

During flooding dirt mixes with drinking water. This dirty water causes diseases such as cholera, to spread quickly through cities.

flash flood sudden flood after heavy rain

VERY DANGEROUS

DRIED UP!

Long periods of dry weather may not seem deadly. But **droughts** cause crops to wither and die. Without food, animals and people starve to death.

drought long period of weather with little or no rainfall

Between the 1960s and 1980s, droughts in Africa killed more than 100,000 people.

WHITEOUT

Blizzards bring whirling snow and icy winds. **Whiteouts** make it hard to see and travellers get lost. Icy roads cause deadly accidents. There are a lot of whiteouts in Iceland.

whiteout blizzard where objects are hard to see

DEADLY *FACT*

Many people die of heart attacks whilst clearing heavy snow.

STRUCK DOWN!

Thunderstorms can have deadly lightning. Lightning strikes can **electrocute** people. Even a lightning strike nearby is hot enough to burn a person.

electrocute injure or kill by electricity

EXTREME RAIN

Monsoons bring much-needed rain to Asia and Africa. But they can also cause deadly floods. These floods destroy homes and crops. People also drown in floodwaters.

DEADLY *FACT*

On 10 March 2009, a monsoon hit Mumbai, India. Just under one metre of rain fell on the city.

monsoon season in hot countries when heavy rain falls

EXTREMELY DANGEROUS

TWISTERS

Tornadoes destroy whatever they touch. These windstorms can spin as fast as 480 kilometres (300 miles) per hour. Strong tornadoes can even suck up people, cars, and buildings.

tornado violent storm with a whirling wind

The U.K. has around 50 tornadoes a year, but they are small and do little damage.

DEADLY HURRICANES

Hurricanes hit coastlines with powerful winds and sheets of rain. Their **storm surges** flood low-lying coasts. People caught in a storm surge can get swept away and drown.

DEADLY *FACT*

Some hurricanes can unleash more than 9 trillion litres of rain a day.

storm surge sudden, strong rush of water that happens as a hurricane moves onto land

TROPICAL DISASTERS

Typhoons and **cyclones** are the same as hurricanes. Typhoons rip through the North Pacific Ocean. Cyclones strike the South Pacific Ocean. Both types of storm kill thousands of people each year.

typhoon violent storm in the North Pacific Ocean

cyclone violent storm in the South Pacific Ocean

DEADLY FACT

A cyclone killed around 300,000 people in Bangladesh in 1970.

HOT FACTS

Heatwaves kill more people each year than any other type of weather. Extremely high **temperatures** can cause **heatstroke**. Whether it's heavy rain or strong winds, weather can turn deadly in an instant!

DEADLY FACT

In 1996, California's Death Valley topped 49 degrees Celsius for 40 days.

heatstroke when a person collapses after being out too long in very hot conditions

GLOSSARY

cyclone violent storm in the South Pacific Ocean

drought long period of weather with little or no rainfall

electrocute injure or kill by electricity

flash flood sudden flood after heavy rain

frostbite when cold temperatures freeze the skin

heatstroke when a person collapses after being out too long in very hot conditions

monsoon season in hot countries when heavy rain falls

storm surge sudden, strong rush of water that happens as a hurricane moves onto land

temperature how hot or cold something is

tornado violent storm with a whirling wind

typhoon violent storm in the North Pacific Ocean

whiteout blizzard where objects are hard to see

FIND OUT MORE

Books

Amazing Planet Earth: Extreme Weather, Jinny Johnson (Franklin Watts, 2009)

Extreme! Storm Chaser: Dicing with the World's Most Deadly Storms, Clive Gifford (A&C Black, 2010)

Eyewitness Companions: Weather, The Met Office (Dorling Kindersley, 2008)

Storm Tracker, Allison Lassieur (Raintree, 2007)

The Weather Book: Why It Happens And Where It Comes From, Diana Craig (Michael O'Mara Books, 2009)

Usborne Beginners: Weather, Catriona Clarke (Usborne Publishing, 2006)

Websites

http://news.bbc.co.uk/cbbcnews/hi/find_out/guides/tech/extreme_weather/
Learn some fascinating facts about the weather.

http://www.weatherwizkids.com/
Try out some interesting weather experiments.

INDEX